Artwork © Jason Pollen
Authors: Harvey Hix
and Patricia Malarcher
Series Editor: Matthew Koumis
Graphic Design: Rachael Dadd
Reprographics: Ermanno Beverari
Printed in Italy

© Telos Art Publishing 2003

Telos Art Publishing
1 Highland Square, Clifton
Bristol BS8 2YB
t/f: +44 (0) 117 923 9124
e: editorial@telos.net
e: sales@telos.net
w: www.telos.net

ISBN 1 902015 73 8 (softback)

A CIP catalogue record for this book
is available from The British Library

Notes
All dimensions are shown in imperial and
metric, height x width x depth.
All work is in private collections unless
otherwise stated.

Photo Credits
E. G. Schempf, Ross Sawyers, Beth
Wickerson

Artist's Acknowledgments
I am grateful to Harvey Hix for
contributing his poetry in the essay he
wrote for this book. Special thanks to
Ny Wetmore, my right hand.

Publisher's Acknowledgements
Thanks to Paul Richardson at Oxford
Brookes University, John Denison, Crivelli
Simone, Valle Marco, Dò Moreno, Briggi
Giuseppe, Nappi Luigi, Filippini Marco,
Coltro Federico, Drapelli Giorgio.

pages 1 & 48:
Terra Ephemera/Summer
1995
printed, painted and
fused silk, dye
46 x 84in (120 x 218cm)

right:
Reawakening
1999
painted, printed and
fused silk, dye
76 x 36in (198 x 94cm)

portfolio collection
Jason Pollen

TELOS

Contents

String Theory
2001
painted and printed silk,
dye, discharge
54 x 144in (140 x 374cm)

Foreword

When I first saw Jason Pollen's textiles at a New York gallery in early the 90's, my attention was immediately riveted. In each work, layers of brilliantly dyed silk particles were invisibly fused to a transparent surface. The pieces of silk were like brush strokes detatched from a canvas, or molecules suspended in a solution. The work was completely straightforward, with all its components in plain sight, nothing concealed, and yet there was an air of mystery about it. That was due, in part, to the lack of any traces of construction – for example, no connecting threads held the particles together. The result was silk that appeared self-sufficient, asserting its colorful voice without the mediation of craft.

In the years following that exhibition, Pollen's extensive research has deepened his knowledge and understanding of the inner life of textiles as well as their surfaces. By widely disseminating what he has found through teaching, lecturing, and writing, he has been instrumental in making surface design a most vital area of contemporary textiles. In being conversant with both the textile industry and studio artists, Pollen commands a view of the field that is exceptionally broad.

In Pollen's recent personal work, surfaces and compositions have become increasingly more complex and more expressive while the scale has expanded. This allows space for light to pass through the fabric, lending it a sense of immateriality. Still there is a continuous thread running through it – textile as itself in a chromatic range that only silk can sing.

Patricia Malarcher
Editor
Surface Design Association

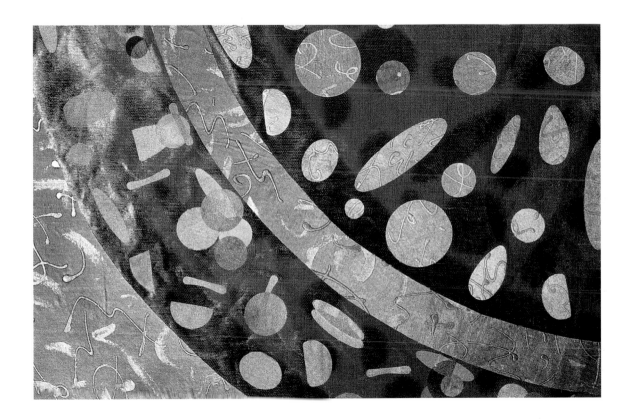

Outbreath (detail)
2001
printed, painted
and fused silk, dye
58 x 58in (151 x 151cm)

Aria
1997
painted and printed silk,
dye, discharge
19 x 77in (49 x 200cm)

Art That Edifies

by Harvey Hix

Art That Edifies

To delight and to teach: Jason Pollen's work lives up to that time-honored artistic standard. Certainly his work delights. Its rich, vibrant colors and sense of pattern are irresistible: their effect is physiological, mood-elevating like a bouquet in a gray office cubicle or a day of sunlight in a dreary February. But Pollen's pieces also edify, not by instructing – asserting facts or imposing values – but by embodying a set of ideals that manifest themselves in different ways in the various distinct bodies of work Pollen has created.

The ideals are consistent with Pollen's experience. Raised in a household saturated with classical music, Jason Pollen was himself a professional dancer until a knee injury at age 23 ended his career; so it is no surprise that animation and immediacy appear as ideals in his art. A traveler, he has lived and worked in India, England, Switzerland, and France, in addition to New York and Kansas City; so the ideal of dialogue seems a logical connection between his life and his art. His formal artistic education was in painting, not fashion design or textiles, a fact that may have helped motivate his pursuit of accumulation and luminosity. In spiritual orientation, he practices Buddhism, consistent with his art's embodiment of elementality and depth. Certain qualities, then, seem to find expression both as aspirations in Pollen's life and as values embodied in his work.

As those qualities concentrate themselves in aspects of Pollen's life (e.g. animation in his love of dance), so they concentrate themselves in bodies of his work. Those bodies are: the drawings Pollen makes incessantly, by the thousands, and from which he derives many of the ideas for his larger works; mosaics in which small swatches of dyed silk (sometimes in simple geometrical forms such as circles or squares, and sometimes in the shape of recognizable small objects, especially leaves and stones) are arrayed on a larger silk base; pieces in which Pollen's own footprints are the focal element; glyphs, in which abstract shapes, often in bright colors, are arrayed as a rebus on an often even brighter background; silver pieces, in which a metallic dye infuses the positive and/or the negative spaces in the patterned arrays that form the composition; and, finally, floor mats, a unique collaboration with the Golden Star corporation in which Pollen's designs are printed with acid dyes on nylon pile fused to a rubber backing.

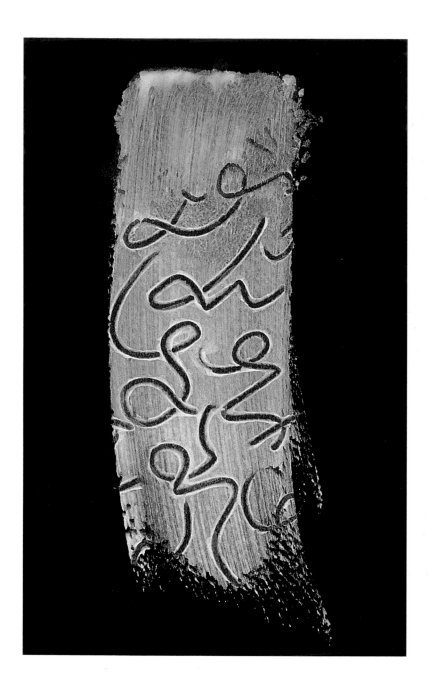

Drawings

Jason Pollen sketches compulsively, and the thousands of resulting drawings perfectly embody one of his ideals, immediacy. Often Pollen makes the drawings on small squares of black construction paper or card stock, but not exclusively: they can be on anything from post-it notes to lined notebook paper to stiffened silk, and they employ a range of colored media. The drawings may be abstract. They may be layered, with an image over a pattern. Or they may be abstract with subtle elements of figuration appearing almost mystically: a barely visible human face, for instance, rising from a background of a similar shade. In any case, they are executed rapidly, arising not from deliberation and rational planning, but from what Dennis Lee calls "kinaesthetic knowing" or "body music." Pollen's drawings are, again in Lee's words, but with a nod to Pollen's own obsession with music and dance, "acts of rhythmic attention." And just as the drawings are executed rapidly, so they are perceived rapidly by the viewer, inviting not analysis but embrace. Immediate, giving themselves wholly, they are art at its most accessible.

left:
Seed Syllables
2002
arches cover stock,
clear gesso, acrylic inks
7 x 7in (18 x 18cm)

page 11:
Paper Chase
2002
nylon pile, acid dye, rubber
24 x 36in (62 x 94cm)

Mosaics

Though they do not number in the thousands like his drawings, Pollen's mosaic pieces do add up to a sizable body of work, distinctive enough in quality that by themselves they would validate Jason Pollen as a significant artist, so it is not only as individual pieces but as a group that Pollen's mosaics embody the ideal of accumulation. One aspect of their origin is technical: Pollen discovered a way of fusing fiber to fiber without stitching or glue, which freed him to assemble small swatches at will on a larger yardage. *Terra Ephemera* (1990), an early example, represents one direction the pieces took. The small bits of fabric are dyed, printed, and painted in the colors of stones, leaves, and twigs, and cut in their shapes. They make the whole

an esker, stream-rounded stones in a cluster the next flash flood will rearrange. Terra Ephemera evokes, in George Oppen's formulation, not

word
nor meaning but the small
selves haunting

us in the stones.

The complement to *Terra Ephemera* is *Terra Ephemera/Crickets* (1992), which also makes no pretense of pattern. Pressed for lineage, it could claim Klimt for kin, but it is less interested in locating the viewer in relation to an art-historical predecessor than in dislocating the viewer from overconfidence in relation to nature.

Terra Ephemera/Crickets
1992
printed, painted and
fused silk, dye
50 x 60in (130 x 156cm)

Terra Firma

1991

printed, painted and
fused silk, dye

26 x 42in (68 x 109cm)

Is it a layer of leaves on the ground, so that I am looking down in the world the work defines? If so, why would the leaves be mostly green? Is it foliage so that I am looking horizontally? If so, am I looking into the foliage or out of it? Am I looking up? Is it leaves at all? In between *Terra Ephemera* and *Terra Ephemera/ Crickets* are other works that blend the two. *Terra Ephemera/Spring* (1993) [p41], *Terra Ephemera/Summer* (1995) [pp1&48], and *Terra Ephemera/ Fall* (1995) [p43], each occupies a vertical rectangle of silk, and each is divided vertically so that approximately two thirds of the area is covered by "stones" and approximately one third by "leaves" or "grass." Again, our relation to nature is called into question. Each piece is "realistic" enough to suggest nature, but the sharpness of the line between rocks and leaves or grass reminds anyone

who has tried to keep a gravel driveway clear of leaves that this is a suggestion of nature, not a presentation of it. Our awareness of nature does not grant us access to it. Pollen's mosaic pieces take one additional direction, into a geometrical abstraction, as in *Dust to Dust* (1990) [p33]. In it two circles emerge from a background of intersecting diamonds/triangles. Donald Judd has pointed out that "two colors on the same surface almost always lie on different depths." In *Dust to Dust*, the red and the blue that form the circles lie nearer the surface than do the browns that compose the triangles/diamonds of the background. The arrangement takes the viewer away from figurative associations. Because the circles are atop rather than beside one another, they do not become breasts or eyes, but retain their more strictly spiritual character.

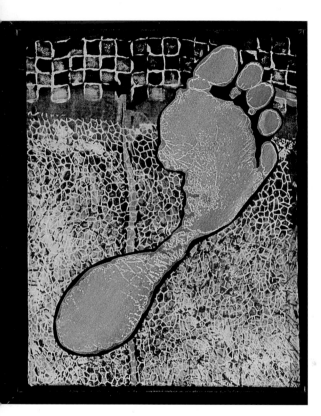

Footprint Pieces

Talk to Jason Pollen long enough, and he will speak of his compulsion to honor the feet. They are humble, bearing us on command, without notice or reward; they are spiritual, providing our most solid contact with the earth, grounding us in ways the eyes and ears cannot. They are vehicles of memory. When Pollen recollects his childhood on Fire Island, he mentions its stones, grasses, and shells: the very items he most often depicts in his work today are the items he felt with his feet as a child. Pollen's footprint pieces, like feet themselves, keep us in touch with elementality, our own and that of the earth. In *Presence of the Other*, the feet – Pollen's own – dominate the composition. Just as feet on the plinth from a long-destroyed Greek statue – or the rough shapes where feet were – can indicate the figure's posture, so the feet in *Presence of the Other* indicate how we stand, able to look at what we leave behind but never wholly out of contact with the earth. Elementality manifests itself in a variety of ways. The feet appear as bodies of water in an aerial photograph, in which case the foreground and background become the two elements water and earth, or as a spirit ascending, in which case they are the other two traditional elements, fire and air. The surface of the cloth on which the feet appear shares their rhagades, takes on their texture, wrinkled and chapped. Its two halves, also like the feet themselves, echo one another but without perfect symmetry.

right:
Walking Meditation Series
1998
silk, dye, printed, painted, stitched,
burnout
34 x 22in (86 x 56cm)

left:
Right Here
1998
painted, printed and fused silk,
dye, potato dextrin
14 x 12in (36 x 31cm)

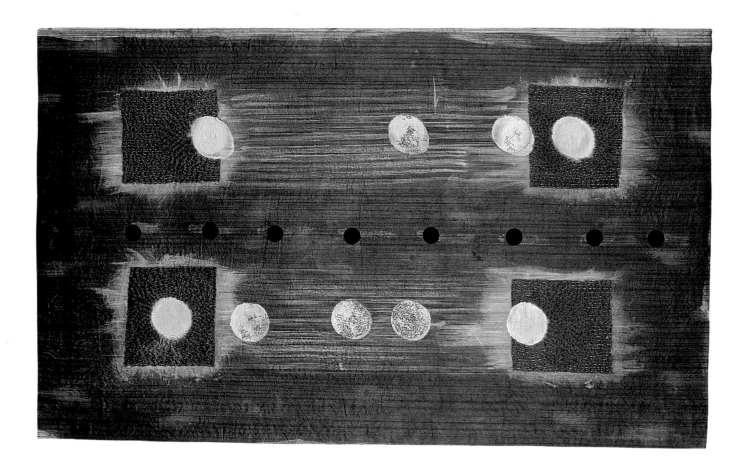

Glyphs

If his mosaics remind viewers that we share our world's elementality, his glyphs place viewers into a dialogue with that world, in each case creating overdetermined visual echoes of linguistic notation systems. In the catalog for his 1997 *Paradox* show, Pollen observes that rhythm and intonation "are common to pictorial as well as spoken and musical languages," and he bases his glyphic works on that commonality.

Works such as *Dance the Dance* (1997) and *Aria* (1997) [p8], use rhythm and intonation to create broad gestural swirls that suggest naskhi Arabic script. In *Dance the Dance* the swirls are broken and fragmented, but in *Aria* the composition is dominated by a single intricate swirl. In both pieces, the swirls themselves consist of parallel lines that suggest those of

the musical staff. Some contemporary composers, such as George Crumb, have altered the staff into circles and other shapes besides straight lines; Pollen has simply set the staff free. Continuing the overdetermination, *Aria* suggests at least one additional language. Its background of horizontal bands of color suggests spectrometry, a language of materials – remember the importance of elementality to the mosaic pieces – that reveals chemical composition.

Other glyphic works, such as *Offering* (1997) [p28], *Cure* (1997), and *Dharma Light* (1997), suggest not Arabic script but the pictographs of Oriental languages, or Egyptian hieroglyphs. Here, too, the linguistic suggestion is over-determined. *Offering,* for example, as if to echo the footprint pieces, edges against, but does not actually employ,

bilateral symmetry. It is divided in half by a vertical row of large characters, and the smaller characters line up on either side nearly in pairs, but the large characters are not themselves symmetrical, and the pairs of characters do not match. In this way, it resembles that most expressive language, facial expression, which also depends on proximity to bilateral symmetry.

In *Eclipse* (2000) [left], the dialogue is not in the script of a human language, but in the mitosis of cells, one cell replicating itself to become two, guided by the language of all life, dna Or at a different scale, the dialogue takes place in the mathematical language Pythagoras thought must create a music of the spheres. Even where the suggestion of language is not obvious, it is present.

Silver Pieces

In a recent series of pieces using metallic organza reactive dye, as in the glyphs that preceded them, Pollen distributes an array of shapes on a silk backing. In the glyphs, the shapes receive emphasis; each shape is unique, complex, and suggestive. In the silver series, the array receives emphasis and the shapes themselves recede. Pollen relies on a very small vocabulary of simple shapes, primarily circles and ellipses, so that the viewer sees not shape but pattern.

Even more importantly, Pollen limits the palette to a small number of colors within a limited range, not in order to diminish their luminosity, but to heighten it. All Pollen's pieces remind us that ours is a world of light, and that human vision is conditioned by light, but these pieces fairly shout the reminder. The reflective quality

of the metallic dye means that we get back not only light as color, in this case silver, but light as light itself. Moreover, the pieces are designed to be hung near but not on the wall, without backing, so that the slightest breeze, as set up by any human presence, starts a complex set of shadows moving in interaction with each other and with the silk.

In *Scent of Rain* (2001), hints remain of the suggestions from earlier pieces. Elementality appears with the weightier bottom third dividing the piece into earth and sky, and the shapes becoming water in an abstract rain. Dialogue recurs with the squiggles that cover the background, and become a coded cursive. But more than ever before, this piece and its sisters shine with light, light, light.

right:
Scent of Rain
2001
painted, printed and stitched silk, dye
44 x 66in (114 x 172cm)

page 20:
Eclipse
2000
painted and printed silk, dye, discharge
24 x 38in (62 x 99cm)

Mats

Jason Pollen's floor mats result from a unique collaboration between art and industry. Taking advantage of the same digital technology and industrial manufacturing processes used to mass-produce rubber-backed indoor/outdoor carpet mats decorated with brand logos for advertising purposes, Pollen has created a series of designs that take the same mats and reinvent them for artistic display. Though Pollen's own hand is limited to the design function, and does not construct the physical piece as in his other works, the mats embody aesthetic ideals no less than does the rest of Pollen's work. In the mats, it is animation that appears central. The physical objects – nylon pile on rubber backing – are quite static, and the mats are functionally static, designed to stay fixedly in place. They need movement, and it is movement that Pollen's designs give them.

Henge (2002) demonstrates this clearly. It seems as though it should be static: the background is gray, the composition is in rows of similar shapes, and the name of the piece confirms the shapes' suggestion of monoliths, one element of whose mystery is how ancient peoples managed to move such heavy objects. Yet, the stones seem to dance. Each is slightly different from the next; the colors, which follow no discernible pattern, add spontaneity; the shaded portion of the stones' outlines is not always on the same side, so the imagined light source moves. Like *Henge*, the related mats *Circle* (2002) and *Square* (2002) are animated subtly. In *Circle*, for instance, the lighter-colored circle in the center of the blue square ground steadies the eye, but the two rows of dots around the circle seem to oscillate back and forth from inner row to outer, and to move in procession around the circle.

Henge (detail)
2002
nylon pile, acid dye, rubber
24 x 36in (62 x 94cm)

CORNWALL COLLEGE
LEARNING CENTRE

Bach on Silk

Jason Pollen's work trusts the transcendent to assert itself in silk and color, as it does in dance and music, those other means, in Yeats's words, "of conversing with eternity." Of all the ways Pollen has stated his ambitions for his art – the wish to transform one thing into another within a single piece, the attempt to create a surface with such depth that it is not a surface at all – perhaps the most definitive formulation is that when he makes a work of art he wants it to be the visual equivalent of a Bach fugue. As a Bach fugue edifies us not by instructing us about the world, but by orienting us to our world as a world of structure and variety and harmonies and complex inter-relationships, so Jason Pollen's art edifies us by orienting us to our world as a world concentrated into the immediate present, a world of rich accumulation, a world composed of and tangible through basic elements, a world that speaks to those who will listen to it and engage it in dialogue, a world that shines, and a restless world of ceaseless motion.

H. L. Hix
Vice President for Academic Affairs
Cleveland Institute of Art

Outbreath
2001
printed, painted and
fused silk, dye
58 x 58in (151 x 151cm)

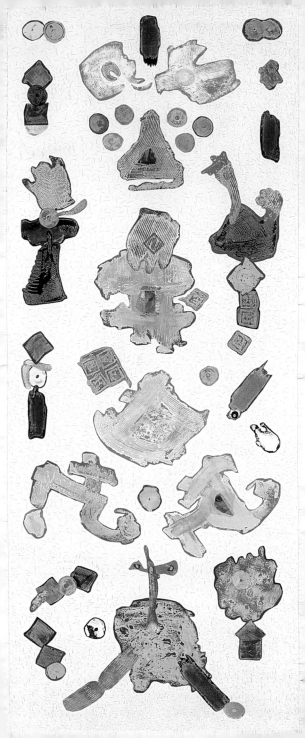

Color Plates

Offering
1997
painted, printed and
stitched silk, dye
57 x 25in (148 x 65cm)

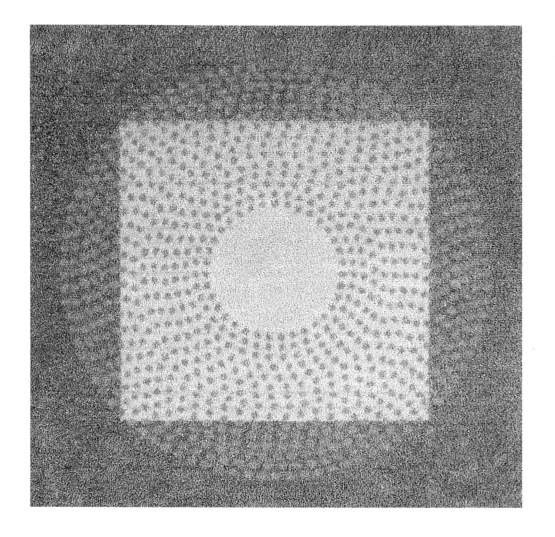

right:
Dust to Dust
1990
printed, painted and
fused silk, dye
17 x 22in (44 x 57cm)

page 30:
Stardust (detail)
2002
nylon pile, acid dye, rubber
36 x 36in (94 x 94cm)

page 31:
Satellite Series/Orange (detail)
2002
nylon pile, acid dye, rubber
24 x 24in (62 x 62cm)

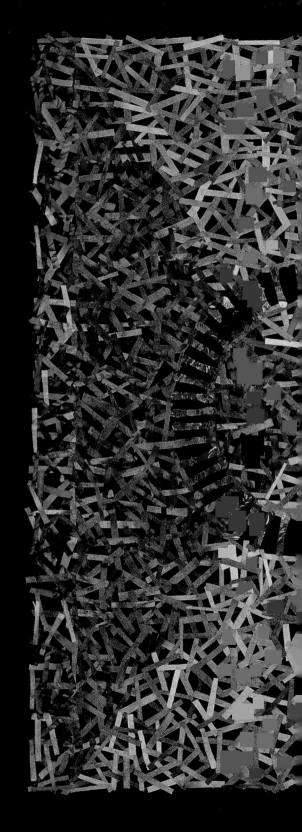

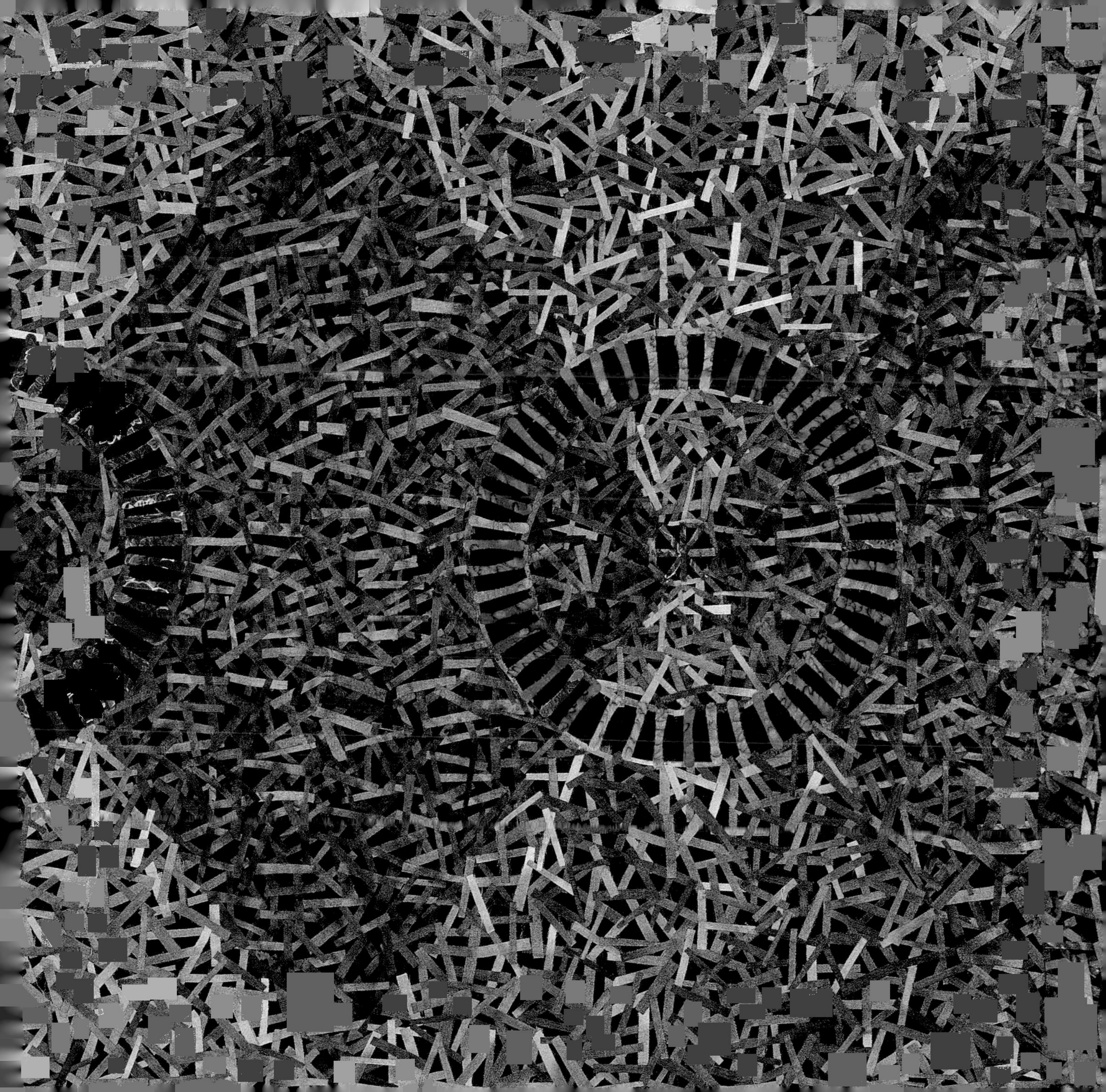

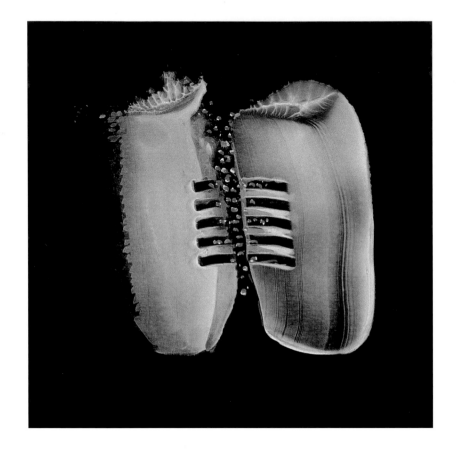

Birth of Blue
2002
arches cover stock,
clear gesso, acrylic inks
7 x 7in (18 x 18cm)

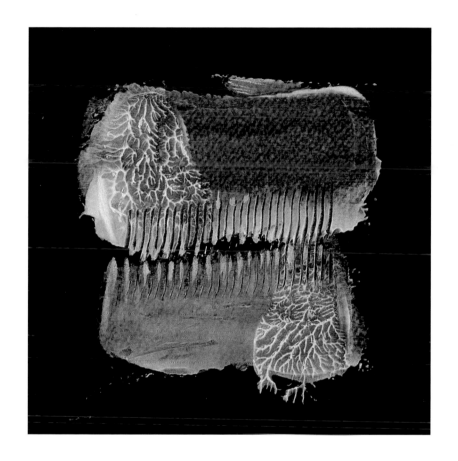

Synapse
2002
arches cover stock,
clear gesso, acrylic inks
7 x 7in (18 x 18cm)

Three Sisters
2002
arches cover stock,
clear gesso, acrylic inks
7 x 7in (18 x 18cm)

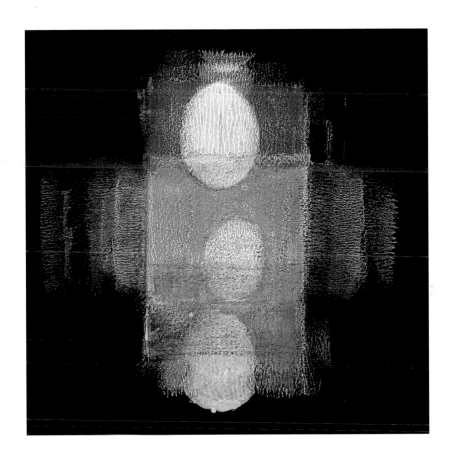

Light Wave
2002
arches cover stock,
clear gesso, acrylic inks
7 x 7in (18 x 18cm)

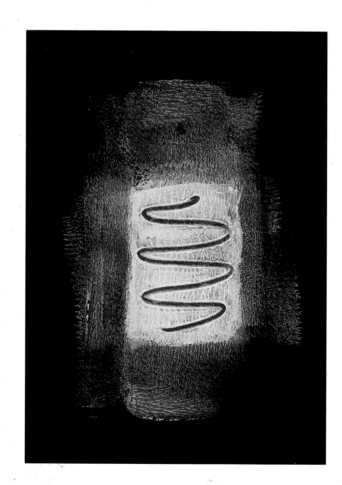

this page:
Arisen
2002
painted silk, dye, discharge
4 x 26in (114 x 68cm)

page 39:
Rising
2002
arches cover stock,
clear gesso, acrylic inks
7 x 7in (18 x 18cm)

above:
Terra Ephemera/Spring
1993
printed, painted and
fused silk, dye
42 x 84in (109 x 218cm)

pages 42 & 43:
Terra Ephemera/Fall
1995
printed, painted and
fused silk, dye
48 x 84in (125 x 218cm)

Biography

Born   1941, New York City

Education

1966   MA in Painting, City College of New York

1964   BFA, City College of New York

Awards

2003   Distinguished Achievement Award, Kansas City Art Institute

2001   Juror's Award, Fiber Focus, Art St. Louis, St. Louis, MO

1992   First Place Winner from the USA, Japan Foundation Sponsored Textile Design Contest

1992   IdeaComo Award for Outstanding Achievement in Printed Textiles,
                 Sponsored by the Government of Italy

1991   Mid-America Arts Alliance Fellowship Winners,
                 Special Purchase Award, H&R Block Foundation

1989   Mid America Arts Alliance/NEA Grant

1987   Missouri Arts Council Grant

1985   Alliance of Independent Colleges of Art (AICA) Grant

Teaching Experience

1997 -   Chair, Fiber Department, Kansas City Art Institute, Kansas City, MO

1983 -   Full Professor, Fiber Department, Kansas City Art Institute, Kansas City, MO

1980 - 1983   Parsons School of Design, New York City

1978 - 1980   Pratt Institute, New York City

1974 - 1976   Royal College of Art, London

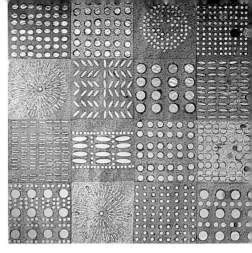

Selected Solo Exhibitions

2003	*Haven*, Dolphin Gallery, Kansas City, MO
	Mats by Jason Pollen, Kansas City, MO
	Recent Work, Wichita Art Center, Wichita, KS
2002	*Mats by Jason Pollen*, H&R Art Space, Kansas City, MO
2000	*Chance of Rain*, Dolphin Gallery, Kansas City, MO
1998	*Mining the Surface*, Temple/Tyler Gallery, Philadelphia, PA
1997	*Paradox*, Leedy-Voulkos Gallery, Kansas City, MO
1995	*Jason Pollen*, Oregon School of Arts and Crafts, Portland OR
1993	*Terra Luminosa*, Dolphin Gallery, Kansas City, MO
1992	*Terra Ephemera*, Kemper Gallery, Kansas City Art Institute, Kansas City, MO
1991	*Perspectives from the Rim*, Bellevue Museum, Seattle, WA

Selected Group Exhibitions

2002	*Gathering Influence*, H&R Block Art Space, Kansas City, MO
2001	*Fiber Focus*, Art St. Louis, Saint Louis, MO
	Off the Record, Johnson County Community College Gallery of Art, Overland Park, KS
2000	*Material Evidence*, Reed Whipple Cultural Center, Las Vegas, NV
	Material Evidence, Sherry Leedy Gallery, Kansas City, MO
1999	*In Progress*, Matthew McFarland Studio, Kansas City, MO
	Dropcloth, COCA, St. Louis, MO
1998	Snyderman Gallery, Philadelphia, PA
	Ten in Textiles, Craft Alliance, St. Louis, MO
1997	*Surface Tension*, Anheuser-Busch Gallery at COCA, St Louis, MO
	Threads, New Jersey Center for the Visual Arts, Summit, NJ
	North Country Studio Conference Exhibition, Bennington College, Bennington, VT
	Surface to Structure, Greenville Museum of Art, Greenville, NC
	Artspace, Raleigh, North Carolina; The Art Gallery,
	Central Piedmont Community College, Charlotte, NC

Selected Group Exhibitions continued

1996	Textile Museum Max Berk, Heidelberg, Germany
	Silk Roads: Roads of Contemporary Art, Central Museum of Textiles, Lodz, Poland
1995	Leedy-Voulkos Gallery, Kansas City, MO
	New Tools, No Limits, Portland State University, Portland, OR
1994	*The Spiritual in Art*, Community Christian Church, Kansas City, MO
1995	Leedy-Voulkos Gallery, Kansas City, MO
	Kyoto Museum, Kyoto, Japan
1993	American Fiber Arts '93, Mendocino Art Center, Mendocino, CA
	Pushing the Boundaries, Evanston Art Center, Evanston, IL
	Year of American Crafts Exhibition, Craft Alliance, St. Louis, MO
1992	*Fiber Art*, Salishan Gallery, Portland, OR
	Natural Influences, Switzer Gallery, Rochester Institute of Technology, Rochester NY
	Hanae Mori Space, Tokyo, Japan
1990	*Splendid Forms: '90*, curated by Jack Lenor Larsen, Bellas Artes Gallery, Santa Fe, New Mexico and New York City

Selected Recent Publications

2003	*Review Magazine*, Kansas City, MO, 'Jason Pollen'
	Kansas City Star Magazine, 'Jason Pollen',
	Fiberarts Magazine, December Issue
2002	*Chicago Tribune*, Sunday, October 20, 'Mats by Jason Pollen',
2002	*Surface Design Association Journal,* Summer issue, 'Surface Design: 25 Years', by Jason Pollen
2000	*Art Textiles of the World*, Matthew Koumis, Telos Art Publishing, London
1999	*Surface Design Journal*, Winter Issue, 'Jason Pollen, Mining the Surface'
1998	*Fiberarts Magazine*, Winter Issue, 'Jason Pollen'
1997	A Catalog of the Solo Exhibition, Leedy-Voulkos Gallery, Kansas City, MO, 'Jason Pollen: Paradox
	Kansas City Home Design, March
1997	*New York Times*, February 23, 'New Dimensions in Working with Fiber,' by William Zimmer
1996	*Fiberarts*, Jan/Feb, 'Connecting with a Moment,' by Catherine S. Amidon

Textile Designer:

Jack Lenor Larsen, New York City;

Jim Thompson Thai Silks Ltd., Bangkok, Thailand;

Liberty of London, London, England;

Perry Ellis, New York City; Oscar de la Renta, New York City;

Yves St. Laurent, Paris, France;

Ungaro, Paris, France;

Lanvin, Paris, France;

Wamsutta, Inc., New York City;

Riverdale-Cohama Fabrics, New York City;

First Edition Wall Coverings, New York City;

Jantzen Swimwear, Los Angeles, CA;

Nieman-Marcus, Dallas, TX;

Hallmark Cards, Inc., Kansas City, MO;

Donna Karan, New York City;

Peruvian Connection, Tonganoxie, KS

Professional

2003 - Present	Design Director, *Mats* by Jason Pollen
1993 - Present	President, Surface Design Association
1995 - 2000	Director, Kansas City Friends of Tibet

Website

www.jasonpollen.com

page 45:
Realignment (detail)
2001
printed, painted and
fused silk, dye
44 x 78in (114 x 203cm)